THE 10

Most Revolutionary Songs

Andrea Cameron

Series Editor
Jeffrey D. Wilhelm

Much thought, debate, and research went into choosing and ranking the 10 items in each book in this series. We realize that everyone has his or her own opinion of what is most significant, revolutionary, amazing, deadly, and so on. As you read, you may agree with our choices, or you may be surprised — and that's the way it should be!

Franklin Watts®

an imprint of

SCHOLASTIC

www.scholastic.com/librarypublishing

A Rubicon book published in association with Scholastic Inc.

Rubicon © 2008 Rubicon Publishing Inc.
www.rubiconpublishing.com

Associate Publishers: Kim Koh, Miriam Bardswich
Project Editor: Amy Land
Editor: Christine Boocock
Creative Director: Jennifer Drew
Project Manager/Designer: Jeanette MacLean
Graphic Designer: Jeanette MacLean

The publisher gratefully acknowledges the following for permission to reprint copyrighted material in this book.

Every reasonable effort has been made to trace the owners of copyrighted material and to make due acknowledgment. Any errors or omissions drawn to our attention will be gladly rectified in future editions.

Cover image: The Rolling Stones–Photo by HARRY GOODWIN/All Action/ KEYSTONE Canada. © Copyright 2001 by All Action Photographer: © HARRY GOODWIN/All Action; all other images istockphoto and shutterstock

Library and Archives Canada Cataloguing in Publication

Cameron, Andrea
  The 10 most revolutionary songs / Andrea Cameron.

Includes index.
ISBN: 978-1-55448-493-5

    1. Readers (Elementary). 2. Readers–Songs–History and criticism.
I. Title. II. Title: Ten most revolutionary songs.

PE1117.C35 2007   428.6   C2007-906865-0

1 2 3 4 5 6 7 8 9 10   10   17 16 15 14 13 12 11 10 09 08

Printed in Singapore

Contents

THE TIMES THEY ARE A-CHANGIN'

What is a revolution? It's an idea or event that changes the way people think. Anything that has a major, sudden, and lasting impact on society qualifies as revolutionary. And, as the above Bob Dylan quote suggests, the 20th century has been a time of huge changes! During this time, the music industry has had its share of revolutionary moments. Whether it's the sound, the lyrics, or the performance, the music that inspires us often breaks the rules. This book is not just about a catchy chorus or a groovy beat. It's about the music that makes us think — the music that moves us.

These songs stirred things up and changed the way people felt. When ranking the songs in this book, we looked at the effect each one had. Some of these songs have powerful and thought-provoking lyrics. Each one inspired some kind of change — musically, politically, or culturally. Many of them provided comfort during times of injustice. A few launched the careers of some of the most famous artists of all time. Finally, these songs all influenced musicians who came after them. They challenged the rules of their genre, and pushed musical boundaries. These rockin' rebels paved the way for music today!

genre: *type or category of music*

WHICH IS THE MOST REVOLUTIONARY SONG OF ALL TIME?

MAY 29, 2006

www.time.com   AOL Keyword: TIME

HERE COMES THE HURRICANE SEASON ■ JERRY BROWN ■ TOURIST SURGERY

TIME

Radical Chicks

They criticized the war and were labeled unpatriotic.
Now THE DIXIE CHICKS are back, betting their careers
on a whole new style. Is America ready?
BY JOSH TYRANGIEL

The debut of "Not Ready to Make Nice" put the Dixie Chicks back in the spotlight. On May 29, 2006, they appeared on the cover of TIME magazine.

TO MAKE NICE

ARTIST: The Dixie Chicks wrote and performed this song.

ALBUM AND YEAR: *Taking the Long Way*, 2006

A REAL REVOLUTION! The Dixie Chicks reinvented themselves as champions of free speech with "Not Ready to Make Nice."

In 2003, the Dixie Chicks were at the top of the music industry. They had the #1 country single on the charts. Their concerts were sold out. They won all kinds of prizes at music awards shows. Their songs dominated country music radio stations. But on March 10, 2003, the all-female group's luck suddenly changed. This was the day that lead singer Natalie Maines decided to speak her mind. During a live performance in London, England, Maines said she was ashamed that President George W. Bush was from her home state of Texas. Bad move! The comment angered many Americans. They accused the Dixie Chicks of being unpatriotic. Within days, the group's music was boycotted all over the United States. People even went so far as to burn their Dixie Chicks CDs in protest!

The band made attempts to apologize. Maines tried to clarify her comment at another concert. She also released an official apology to all fans who had been offended. However, nothing slowed the attacks. So instead of continuing to say they were sorry, the Dixie Chicks decided to try something new. They used the airwaves to get their message across. In March 2006, they released the single "Not Ready to Make Nice." The song directly addressed the controversy. Despite its lack of radio play, the song became one of the most downloaded tracks on the Internet. People liked the fact that the song supported the idea of free speech. It also turned these country crooners into rockers!

---

unpatriotic: *showing lack of loyalty to one's country*
boycotted: *refused to buy or use something based on moral beliefs*

NOT READY TO MAKE NICE

ARTISTS' BIOS

The Dixie Chicks formed in Dallas, Texas, in 1989. The group was known for its bluegrass music and colorful cowgirl outfits. Bluegrass uses acoustic instruments such as banjos and fiddles. It is based on Celtic music. In 1995, lead singer Laura Lynch was replaced by spunky Natalie Maines. The Texas trio has been playing together ever since. The group first became big in the independent scene. It wasn't long before they exploded into the mainstream music market.

STORY BEHIND THE SONG

This song directly addresses what the band went through after Maines's controversial comment. In the song, the Dixie Chicks ask, "And how in the world can the words that I said/Send somebody so over the edge"? From death threats to boycotts, the band members faced a lot of abuse after the event. According to the band, the song was written in response to the pain and fear they felt. Lines like "I'm not ready to back down" make their feelings clear. The Dixie Chicks weren't angry at "the war or the president — or at their many fans who deserted them," according to journalist Steve Kroft who interviewed the band in 2006. "[They were angry] about the hatred and narrow-minded intolerance they encountered for expressing an opinion."

Celtic music: *genre based on traditional Scottish, Irish, or Welsh music*
independent scene: *section of the music industry operating without the help of major record labels*
intolerance: *unwillingness to recognize and respect differences in opinions or beliefs*

MEANINGFUL MUSIC

There's no doubt about it — "Not Ready to Make Nice" was a big risk. After the "London incident" (that's how the Dixie Chicks refer to Maines's 2003 statement) the band's sales plummeted. Their new single challenged the traditional sound and ideals of country music. The emotional lyrics clearly showed the hurt and betrayal the Dixie Chicks felt after being attacked for speaking their minds. This was their song of protest. Amazingly enough, it connected with people everywhere, and it brought the group back into the spotlight!

? "Not Ready to Make Nice" wasn't the apology many people thought it would be. Are you surprised the band responded angrily to what happened? How would you have responded and why?

Winners of Best Record of the Year, Best Album of the Year, Best Song of the Year, Best Country Performance by a Duo or Group with Vocal, and Best Country Album, the Dixie Chicks show off their Grammy Awards in 2007.

? According to the U.S. Constitution, all Americans have the right to free speech. However, the Dixie Chicks were attacked when their lead singer spoke her mind. Do you think Natalie Maines should have said what she did? Explain.

Quick Fact

In 2006, a documentary movie titled *Shut Up and Sing* was released. It documented the aftermath of Natalie Maines's anti-George Bush statement. The title of the film can be found in the lyrics of "Not Ready to Make Nice."

10   9   8   7   6

WEIGHT OF WORDS

"Just so you know ... we're ashamed that the President of the United States is from Texas." See how these 16 words changed the world's opinion of the Dixie Chicks in the following chart.

BEFORE	BACKLASH	NEW BEGINNINGS
The Dixie Chicks won three awards at the 2002 Grammy Awards, including the award for Best Country Album.	Radio stations hosted "chicken toss" events. They encouraged fans to destroy Dixie Chicks CDs.	At the 2006 Grammy Awards, the Dixie Chicks won all five categories in which they were nominated. "Not Ready to Make Nice" won Best Song of the Year. The group also won Album of the Year.
Tickets to the Dixie Chicks' "Top of the World" tour sold out within hours.	Concert attendance dropped by half. Sales of the album *Home* dropped by 42 percent.	In response to the "London incident" the band started to write its own music. They created the album *Taking the Long Way*.
Their single "Travelin' Soldier" was #1 on the charts. Houston country station KKBQ-FM played the song an average of 12 times a day.	Their #1 song "Travelin' Soldier" dropped off the charts within two weeks.	The 2006 documentary *Shut Up and Sing* won six awards at North American film festivals. Many of these were audience awards.

Quick Fact

The Dixie Chicks caused a stir when they appeared on the cover of *Entertainment Weekly* in May 2003. Some of the names they were called after Maines's comment, such as "traitors," "opinionated," and "big mouth," were written across their bodies.

The Expert Says...

"One country and one form of music aren't enough to contain [the Dixie Chicks] or stifle their passion. They'll sing but they won't shut up. That seems downright American."

— Richard Corliss, *TIME* magazine

stifle: *suppress; crush*

Take Note

"Not Ready to Make Nice" is #10 on our list. Its success proved that the Dixie Chicks are unstoppable. Their sound challenged the rules of country music. Their powerful lyrics also influenced others to stand up for what they believe in. The Dixie Chicks have been so influential that in 2006, they were listed on *TIME* magazine's list of The People Who Shape Our World.
- The tagline for the movie *Shut Up and Sing* is "Freedom of speech is fine as long as you don't do it in public." What do you think this means?

NEIL YOUNG
SOUTHERN MAN

After "Southern Man" was released, rock group Lynyrd Skynyrd released "Sweet Home Alabama" in defense of the South.

MAN

ARTIST: Neil Young

ALBUM AND YEAR: *After the Gold Rush*, 1970

A REAL REVOLUTION! Neil Young's "Southern Man" is a blunt criticism of racism in the American South.

Neil Young is known for his country-rock sound and powerful songwriting abilities. So when he released "Southern Man" in 1970, the song's no-nonsense protest lyrics came as no surprise. "Southern Man" is about racism. The song attacks the poor treatment of African Americans in the American South.

So, what inspired a Canadian singer to write a song about the American South? Legend has it that Young wrote "Southern Man" after a trip to Alabama. One night while in Alabama, Young was attacked by two men. They didn't like his long hair or hippie style. Frustrated by what had happened, Young wrote a song criticizing racism and prejudice of all kinds.

Throughout his career, Young has "continually explored new musical territory," according to writer Stephen Erlewine. He has never shied away from controversial topics. Today, many of his songs have an anti-war message. With "Southern Man," Young wanted to focus on the issue of racism.

ARTIST BIO

Neil Young was born in Ontario, Canada, on November 12, 1945. After his parents divorced, Young moved to Winnipeg with his mother. He performed with numerous high-school rock bands and folk groups before joining the Mynah Birds in 1966. A year later, Young moved to Los Angeles. There, he formed a band called Buffalo Springfield with some fellow musicians. "Apart from the Byrds, no other American band had as great an impact on folk rock and country rock … than Buffalo Springfield," according to Stephen Erlewine.

? Neil Young once said that his life philosophy was to "always move forward." He believes that each one of us needs "to keep searching for whatever it is that interests you." Do you agree with this philosophy? Explain why or why not.

Young owes his success to natural talent! The singer/songwriter has only had one music lesson in his entire life. "I figured out what to do with a guitar pretty quick on my own," he once said.

STORY BEHIND THE SONG

This song's lyrics talk about racism and slavery, asking, "Southern man when will you pay them back?" Lyrics like these didn't go down too well with a lot of people from the South. But they certainly got people's attention! "Young was writing about segregation and the civil rights struggle," according to Erlewine. Soon after "Southern Man" was released, a band called Lynyrd Skynyrd wrote a response song called "Sweet Home Alabama." In this song, Lynyrd Skynyrd sang positively about the South. Lead singer Ronnie Van Zant said that he felt "Neil was shooting all the ducks in order to kill one or two."

? Ronnie Van Zant felt that Neil Young was attacking everyone from the South in his song, not just the ones guilty of racism. Do you think Neil Young was unfairly targeting people from the South? Explain.

MEANINGFUL MUSIC

"Southern Man" is blunt and to the point in its criticism of the racist behavior of some Americans. The song was released near the end of the American Civil Rights Movement. During this period, many laws were passed to end racial segregation. Despite these laws, racism was still widespread. Even today, not everyone accepts that all people are equal, so the song's message is still relevant. Both "Southern Man" and "Sweet Home Alabama" sparked intense conversations about these issues.

segregation: *act of separating people of different races, classes, or ethnic groups*

Quick Fact

In 1982, Neil Young was inducted into the Canadian Music Hall of Fame. He has been inducted into the Rock and Roll Hall of Fame twice — in 1995 as a solo artist and in 1997 as a member of Buffalo Springfield.

10   **9**   8   7   6

North VS. South

Listening to the mellow rhythm of "Southern Man," it's hard to imagine that it created such controversy. But the song's lyrics are critical of America's history of slavery and oppression. Lynyrd Skynyrd's response also had audiences talking. Both Lynyrd Skynyrd and Neil Young denied there was ever any real tension between them. This comparison chart will help you decide if it was all in fun or a real feud!

Bad Blood?

"As much as we loved his songs, when he wrote about 'Alabama and bullwhips crackin'' we had to answer with 'Sweet Home Alabama.'"

— **Gary Rossington, Lynyrd Skynyrd**

"Don't condemn Southerners now for what their ancestors did." This was Lynyrd Skynyrd's issue with "Southern Man" according to *Glide* magazine writer Ross Warner.

"['Southern Man'] offended many Southerners by seeming to accuse all people born in the South of being intolerant racists. … Southerners were ecstatic when Skynyrd defended their honor."

— **Marley Brant, author of** *The Lynyrd Skynyrd Story*

In Good Fun?

"We wrote 'Alabama' as a joke. We didn't even think about it — the words just came out that way."

— **Ronnie Van Zant, Lynyrd Skynyrd**

"Oh, they didn't really put me down … I think 'Sweet Home Alabama' is a great song."

— **Neil Young**

Lynyrd Skynyrd's lead singer, Ronnie Van Zant, wore a Neil Young T-shirt on the cover of the band's 1977 album, *Street Survivors*.

Quick Fact

In 2003, American music channel VH1 named the Neil Young versus Lynyrd Skynyrd controversy one of the "Top 40 Celebrity Feuds" of all time.

The Expert Says...

"['Southern Man' captures] the sound of what happens when people rise up and claim what is rightfully theirs."

— Denise Sullivan, music writer, allmusic.com

Take Note

"Southern Man" heats up the #9 spot. In this song, Neil Young showed the power of free speech — he spoke his mind and made people listen up! The song spoke of the cruelty of racism, so it ranks higher than "Not Ready to Make Nice."

• Was "Sweet Home Alabama" seriously defending the South against "Southern Man"? Or do you think Lynyrd Skynyrd meant it as more of a joke? Read the lyrics of both songs and decide.

5   4   3   2   1

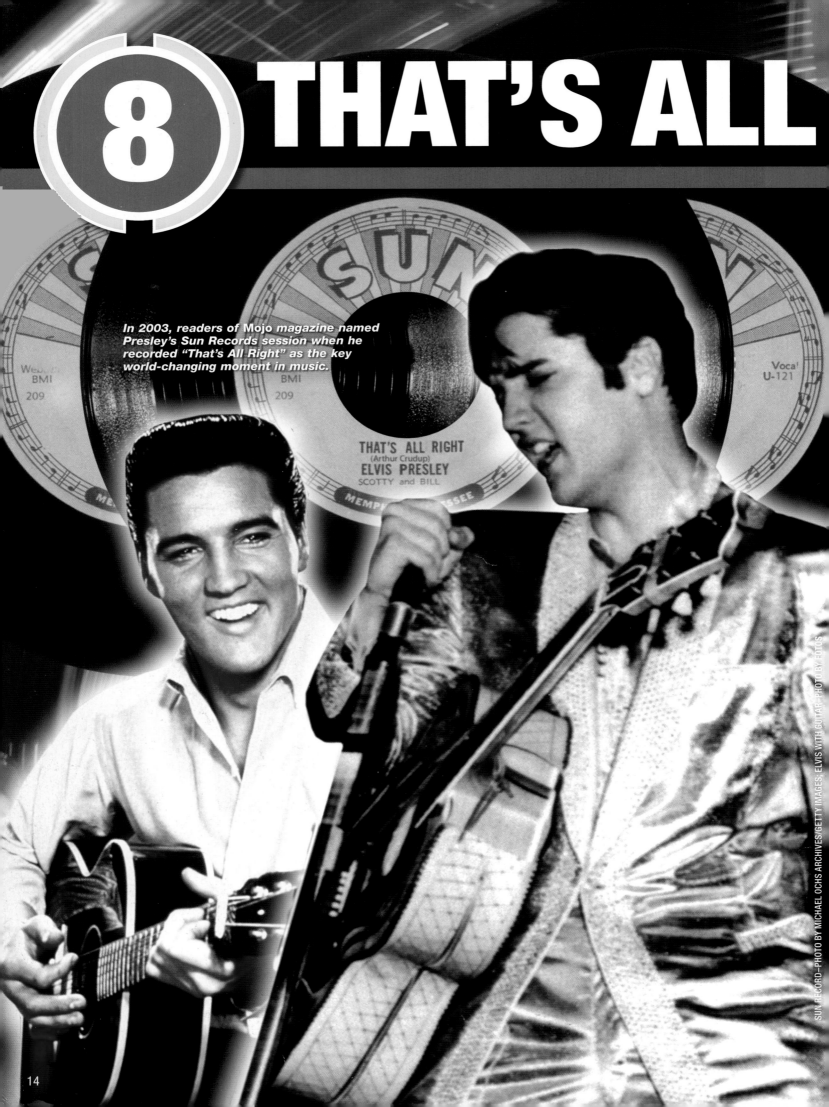

(8) THAT'S ALL

In 2003, readers of *Mojo* magazine named Presley's Sun Records session when he recorded "That's All Right" as the key world-changing moment in music.

THAT'S ALL RIGHT
(Arthur Crudup)
ELVIS PRESLEY
SCOTTY and BILL

RIGHT

ARTIST: This song was written by blues singer Arthur Crudup. It became famous thanks to Elvis Presley's recording.

ALBUM AND YEAR: 1954

A REAL REVOLUTION! No one can deny that Elvis is "The King." His rise to the top started with what was possibly the world's first rock and roll song — "That's All Right."

So you know Elvis Presley is "The King," but just how big is he? He has the most Top 40 hit songs, the most Top 10 hits, and the most consecutive #1 hits in music history! As if that's not enough, he's also credited with breathing life into rock and roll.

When Presley was 18, he was working as a truck driver in Memphis, Tennessee. But he had a passion for music that he couldn't ignore. Wanting to break into the music scene, the ambitious singer paid to record two songs at the Memphis Recording Service. This was a business owned by record producer and owner of Sun Records, Sam Phillips. When Presley returned to record two more songs, he was in for a surprise. Phillips was listening! At the time, Phillips had been looking for a way to popularize African-American music among white audiences. He felt that he could popularize soul, blues, and gospel sounds with white audiences if he presented them in the right way. "If I could find a white man who had the [African-American] sound and the [African-American] feel, I could make a billion dollars." Once Phillips heard Elvis Presley, the billion dollars didn't seem far behind!

On July 5, 1954, Presley recorded his debut single, "That's All Right." "Audience response was overwhelming," according to *Rolling Stone* magazine.

Soul, rhythm and blues, and gospel music were popular among African-American audiences long before Elvis Presley. Why do you think these genres didn't catch on with white audiences until Presley came along? What does this tell you about racism at the time?

THAT'S ALL RIGHT

ARTIST BIO

Elvis Aaron Presley was born in 1935 in the small town of Tupelo, Mississippi. Living in Mississippi, Presley was influenced by many styles of music. He listened to country music on the radio and sang gospel music in church. The year after his graduation, Presley took his first step toward becoming "The King." This was the year that he recorded five singles with Sun Records. "For quite a few scholars, they remain not only Elvis's best singles, but the best rock and roll ever recorded," according to music writer Richie Unterberger.

> **?** Presley didn't write most of the songs that he was famous for performing. Does this change the way you feel about him as an artist? Does a song's fame depend more on the creator or the performer? Explain.

STORY BEHIND THE SONG

Before Presley made it famous, "That's All Right" was recorded as a blues tune by the man who wrote it — Arthur "Big Boy" Crudup. Crudup was a guitar player and singer/songwriter. He had recording contracts with several studios over the course of his career. He has even been called the father of rock and roll! Despite his talents, Crudup never became truly famous. As an African-American musician he wasn't given the same opportunities as white performers. One of his biggest claims to fame is the fact that he wrote three of the songs that Elvis Presley made famous. Presley first recorded "That's All Right" with guitarist Scotty Moore and bassist Bill Black. The trio gave the song what *Rolling Stone* magazine has called a "fast, lusty new style."

The Expert Says...

" You don't think of Elvis as political, but that is politics: changing the way people see the world. "

— Bono, lead singer of U2

MEANINGFUL MUSIC

Rock and roll is a style of music that has been influenced by everything from blues and country to R&B. "That's All Right" wasn't the first song to combine these styles. However, it was the first to really capture what rock and roll was all about. "Elvis provided all the youth, energy, and swagger that made the birth of rock and roll so memorable," according to the BBC. "That's All Right" brought the sounds of African-American musicians to a white audience. The song was innovative. It also scandalized the older generation! In 2005, *Rolling Stone* chose "That's All Right" as the song that started the rock and roll revolution!

R&B: *rhythm and blues music*
innovative: *cutting edge; ahead of the times*

> **?** Despite his fame, Presley received some harsh criticisms in his day. After appearing at the Grand Ole Opry, Presley was told he should go back to truck driving! But he didn't. What does this tell you about Presley?

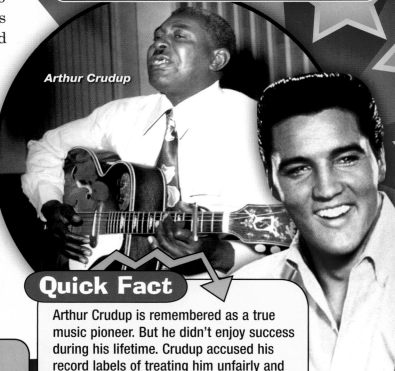

Arthur Crudup

Quick Fact

Arthur Crudup is remembered as a true music pioneer. But he didn't enjoy success during his lifetime. Crudup accused his record labels of treating him unfairly and paying him less than he deserved for his music. Crudup was paid so little as a recording artist that he held other jobs to supplement his income.

There's Only One ELVIS

At the height of his fame, Elvis Presley represented everything that was cool, new, and daring. Read this list of things that made him "The King."

The Attitude

Presley combined rebellion and vulnerability into one. This made him appeal to both male and female fans. His raised eyebrow and curled lip let everyone know that rock and roll was here to stay ... whether they liked it or not.

The Voice

Presley sang a mix of gospel, country, and rock and roll. His rich voice embodied the sound of the American South and the attitude of rock. In 2004, Bono of U2 perfectly described his voice as "elastic."

The Moves

After he started to perform, Presley became known as much for his wild stage shows as for his sound! "Some people tap their feet, some people snap their fingers, and some people sway back and forth. I just sorta do 'em all together, I guess," Presley once said. Presley's swiveling hips caused plenty of controversy and became his signature move.

The Music

Many people feel that "That's All Right" was the true birth of the rock genre. According to music channel VH1, "[Presley] was the musician most responsible for popularizing rock and roll on an international level." He was also the "single most important figure in American 20th-century popular music."

Take Note

"That's All Right" rocks into the #8 spot. This song launched Elvis Presley's career. "That's All Right" also signaled the birth of rock and roll — one of the world's most revolutionary music genres! From day one, rock and roll was unconventional and controversial. It has spoken to young people everywhere, and the genre continues to be popular today.

- Some critics claim that Presley stole music from African-American artists. In your opinion, did he hurt or help African-American music by bringing it into the mainstream? Explain.

5   4   3   2   1

NIRVANA

SMELLS LIKE TEEN SPIRIT

Nirvana performed at the MTV "Live and Loud" show in Seattle in 1993.

TEEN SPIRIT

ARTIST: Written and performed by Nirvana members Kurt Cobain, Krist Novoselic, and Dave Grohl.

ALBUM AND YEAR: *Nevermind*, 1991

A REAL REVOLUTION! This angry, gritty-sounding song burst through the glossy pop scene of the 1980s. It opened the door for underground punk and alternative music.

It was 1991 when record producer Butch Vig first popped "Smells Like Teen Spirit" into a tape player. It wasn't a great recording. Vig couldn't really make out the words. But he decided to include it on Nirvana's second album, *Nevermind*, anyway. Vig never imagined that the song, named after a brand of girl's deodorant, would one day be named the ninth greatest song of all time by *Rolling Stone* magazine.

"Smells Like Teen Spirit" is loud, angry, and catchy. It was the first single off *Nevermind* and it became an instant success. It wasn't only successful with grunge fans either. This song was catchy enough to appeal to fans of all types of music. "Smells Like Teen Spirit" was a huge crossover hit. "Nirvana's second album turned out to be the place where alternative rock crashed into the mainstream," wrote music journalist Stephen Erlewine. "Nirvana pulled [pop, rock, punk, and indie music] all together, creating a sound that was both fiery and melodic."

"Smells Like Teen Spirit" came to symbolize the grunge movement. The song became an "anthem for apathetic kids," according to *TIME* magazine. The cardigans and ratty plaid shirts worn by lead singer Kurt Cobain became the uniform of a generation. This song sparked the grunge revolution of the '90s.

grunge: *style of rock music featuring loud, distorted guitars and moody lyrics*
apathetic: *feeling or showing a lack of interest or concern*

SMELLS LIKE TEEN SPIRIT

ARTISTS' BIOS

Nirvana was formed in 1987. The band's first album, *Bleach*, cost just over $600 to produce. Most albums cost thousands of dollars to put together! *Bleach* sold more than 35,000 copies. It also caught the attention of major record labels. It wasn't long before the band's second album really got them noticed! Unfortunately, lead singer Kurt Cobain had difficulties dealing with the band's instant fame. His struggles with depression and addiction influenced the band's music. They ultimately led to his death in 1994.

STORY BEHIND THE SONG

"Smells Like Teen Spirit" was inspired by the music of the Pixies. This alternative band is known for songs that mix punk and pop in melodic, unique ways. Cobain has said that with this song, he set out to compose "the ultimate pop song." He tried to capture all the angst of alternative rock in a catchy tune. Cobain came up with the title after a friend spray-painted "Kurt smells like Teen Spirit" on his wall as a joke. Cobain was unaware that Teen Spirit was actually a deodorant brand until months after the single was released.

angst: *feeling of dread, anxiety, or anguish*

Nirvana's music often explored the frustration of youth. Why are teen years such a struggle for so many people?

The Expert Says...

" This was clearly the start of something new, something fresh, something young. ... [A] pop-culture movement, led by Cobain's 'Teen Spirit,' altered the American landscape. "

— Jamie Allen, writer for *Salon* magazine

MEANINGFUL MUSIC

When *Nevermind* was released, "Smells Like Teen Spirit" was quickly recognized as revolutionary. It is "an acerbic rant against those who follow the herd," according to writer Jamie Allen. The kids of Generation X were dissatisfied, angry, and unsure of what to do with their lives. The song's lyrics, "Here we are now, entertain us," seemed to put into words what they were thinking. This lyric made it clear that kids weren't being fulfilled by what pop culture offered them. Cobain seemed to understand that America's youth was ready to be mentally and emotionally stimulated. The song also signaled a shift in musical tastes. It was "the fault line separating the 'alternative,' grunge era of the early '90s from the 'hair-band' era of the '80s," according to writer Joe Queenan.

acerbic: *harsh; cutting; bitter*
Generation X: *in the 1990s, a term for teenagers and young adults*
fault line: *split; divide*

Quick Fact

In 1992, *Nevermind* began to sell thousands of copies a week. It knocked Michael Jackson's comeback album, *Dangerous*, from the top spot on the Billboard charts.

Krist Novoselic (left), Kurt Cobain, and Dave Grohl, photographed in 1991

GRUNGE GUIDE

Grunge existed before Nirvana, but the group is credited with popularizing the movement. Learn more about the fashion, the feeling, and the genre of grunge in this list.

1 TEENAGE ANGST

Grunge was all about the moody, angry attitude of a generation. Cobain was able to tap into this feeling. He could flip between weariness and rage within a single song. This represented the confused feelings of Generation X.

2 SEATTLE

Grunge is sometimes called the Seattle Sound. This is because most of the bands who originated this style came from the Seattle, Washington, area. "Smells Like Teen Spirit" was first performed there on April 17, 1991. If country music was born in Memphis, grunge was born in Seattle.

3 STYLE

The 1980s were all about big hair, leather pants, and flashy pop stars. Kurt Cobain was the exact opposite of these trends. He wore jeans with holes in the knees, sneakers, and cardigans. Nirvana's appeal stood in contrast to the "perfection" of the pop divas and glam rockers of the time.

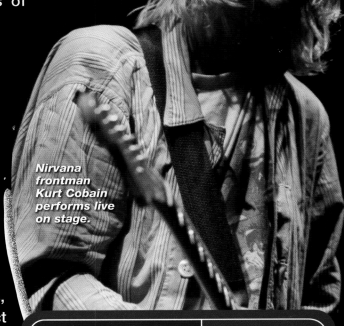

Nirvana frontman Kurt Cobain performs live on stage.

Quick Fact

Amazingly enough, Kurt Cobain grew to hate the song that made him famous. He's been compared to John Lennon because of their shared distrust of fame. Both artists seemed to reject fame as they became celebrities.

Take Note

"Smells Like Teen Spirit" rages into the #7 spot. This song revolutionized the music industry. Before it, nobody thought that an alternative band could rule the charts. Afterward, alternative music was all people wanted to hear. Nirvana did for grunge what Elvis did for rock and roll. Since Nirvana wrote all of their own songs and lyrics, they rank higher.

• Was it a good thing for "alternative" music to go mainstream or do you think something was lost in the process? Explain.

5   4   3   2   1

(6) (I CAN'T GET NO)

The ROLLING STONES

Rolling Stone *magazine recently chose "Satisfaction" as the #2 greatest song of all time. In 2000, the song came in at #1 on VH1's list of greatest rock and roll songs ever!*

SATISFACTION

ARTIST: "(I Can't Get No) Satisfaction" was written by Rolling Stones band members Mick Jagger and Keith Richards.

ALBUM AND YEAR: *Out of Our Heads*, 1965

A REAL REVOLUTION! This song, "Satisfaction" for short, introduced a new sound to rock and roll. As Mick Jagger once said in an interview, this song expressed the spirit of the times.

It all started with a riff that came to Keith Richards in a dream. *Newsweek* called this riff "five notes that shook the world." The Rolling Stones put the "rock" in rock and roll with the release of "Satisfaction." Their edgy new sound made them an instant hit — and "Satisfaction" was just the beginning.

In 1965, "Satisfaction" became the Rolling Stones' first hit song in the United States. Many people immediately compared them to the Beatles. However, it quickly became obvious the two bands were very different. Though the Beatles started out as a polite and clean-cut band, the Rolling Stones were rebels from day one!

"Satisfaction" was at the top of the charts for four weeks. Its cutting lyrics and gritty sound gave the band an edge that hadn't been heard before in rock and roll. Mick Jagger, the lead singer of the band, said this song was about his "view of the world" and his "frustration with everything." The song's rebellious spirit and innovative style make it one of the most revolutionary songs of all time.

riff: *short musical phrase, often repeated*

(I CAN'T GET NO) SATISFACTION

? Many musicians say they are as close to members of their bands as to their families. What family qualities may have helped the Rolling Stones stay together for 40 years?

ARTISTS' BIOS

Formed in 1962, the Rolling Stones originally had six members. From day one, Mick Jagger and Keith Richards were the band's primary songwriters. The Rolling Stones "pioneered the gritty, hard-driving blues-based rock and roll that came to define hard rock," says writer Stephen Erlewine. After an eight-month gig at a club in London, the Stones got a record deal with Decca Records. They were soon part of the "British Invasion" started by the Beatles. But as Erlewine writes, "It wasn't until the group released '(I Can't Get No) Satisfaction' in the summer of 1965 that they were elevated to superstars."

STORY BEHIND THE SONG

As the story goes, it was Keith Richards who first dreamed up "Satisfaction." He has said that one night in May 1965, he woke from a deep sleep and heard the music for the song in his head. He quickly picked up his guitar and recorded the song on a nearby tape recorder. Mick Jagger wrote the lyrics the next day. "Satisfaction" was the first Stones single to hit #1 in both Britain and America. According to the Rock and Roll Hall of Fame, "Many consider it the all-time greatest rock and roll song."

Quick Fact

The Stones are "the longest-lived continuously active" rock group in history. In 2007, their "A Bigger Bang Tour" was named the world's most successful music tour by the *Guinness Book of World Records*.

Mick Jagger and Keith Richards perform at a Rolling Stones press conference in 2005.

MEANINGFUL MUSIC

The Rolling Stones' reputation for rebellious, bad-boy behavior went hand in hand with the sound they pioneered. Other bands at the time were creating catchy songs. These were tame as far as content and sound. "Satisfaction" was loud and had a real message. According to Jagger, the song was about his frustration with consumerism. The song criticizes people who believe that material possessions will make them happy. The song inspired other artists to write more personal lyrics. It "is impossible to hear any of the groups that followed [the Rolling Stones] without detecting some sort of influence," writes Erlewine.

? Mick Jagger once said that this song captures the spirit of alienation. Alienation is a feeling of isolation or of being withdrawn from society. In what ways do some people feel alienated today? Explain the reasons why.

BATTLE OF THE BANDS!

 The British Invasion of the 1960s increased interest in everything British! The Beatles started it all, but the Rolling Stones stole some of their thunder. Check out the details of the rivalry in the following chart.

	THE BEATLES	The ROLLING STONES
APPEARANCE	When they first shot to fame, the Beatles performed in similar, clean-cut suits. They also cut their hair in the same shaggy style.	The Stones were sloppy and unkempt. They represented the "darker, scruffier … side of rock and roll," according to the Rock and Roll Hall of Fame.
PERFORMANCE STYLE	The Beatles didn't dance. For the most part, they stood and sang. They also bowed together at the end of each performance.	Mick Jagger had crazy moves! They weren't entirely original — African-American dancers had used them in the past. But Jagger brought them to a new audience. The band had a less choreographed approach to live performances.
INFLUENCES	The Beatles were influenced by the blues. John Lennon has said that Elvis was a major inspiration. The Beatles took the blues and injected them with catchy pop sounds.	The Stones were also strongly influenced by the blues. But they mixed the blues with a guitar-heavy rock sound.
LONGEVITY	This band broke up after 10 years together. The members went in different directions.	The Stones are still together and performing more than 40 years after the band was formed.

The Expert Says…

" ['Satisfaction' was] one of the defining records of its era, reaching #1 around the globe and establishing the Rolling Stones as the second-biggest band in the world, behind only the Beatles. "

— Richie Unterberger, music writer

Take Note

"Satisfaction" takes the #6 spot. Both the Rolling Stones and Nirvana were reckless and restless. However, "Satisfaction" brought a rebellious mood to rock that hadn't existed before. The Rolling Stones have also had incredible longevity. Their revolution is still going strong!
• Why do you think that the more parents hated the Stones, the more teens loved them?

5   4   3   2   1

5 IMAGINE

The "Imagine" mosaic sits in the Strawberry Fields section of New York City's Central Park. On October 9, 1985, this section of the park was dedicated to John Lennon's memory.

WAR IS OVER!

IMA

ARTIST: John Lennon wrote and performed the song "Imagine."

ALBUM AND YEAR: *Imagine*, 1971

A REAL REVOLUTION! Lennon's beautifully crafted melody and plain-spoken lyrics made "Imagine" an anthem for world peace.

John Lennon rose to fame as a member of one of the world's greatest bands. As a Beatle, he was at the forefront of the British Invasion. A guitarist, singer, and songwriter, Lennon wrote most of the group's songs with fellow Beatle Paul McCartney. Lennon's rise to fame with the Beatles was amazing. Even more amazing is the fact that John Lennon's greatest claim to fame may be a song he wrote as an independent artist. "Imagine" is "Lennon's greatest musical gift to the world," according to *Rolling Stone* magazine. Written in 1971, the song is a universal call for peace.

When Lennon wrote this song, the United States was at war in Vietnam and Laos. Lennon was a passionate peace activist. He wanted to spread a message of peace through his music. According to Lennon's widow Yoko Ono, "Imagine" was "just what John believed — that we are all one country, one world, one people. He wanted to get that idea out." In this song, Lennon asks us all to imagine a world without war or conflict. By simply asking, John Lennon made people believe that this world was possible. "Imagine" has a powerful message of peace. The song has crossed cultural, racial, and geographic boundaries.

IMAGINE

ARTIST BIO

Lennon was born in Liverpool, England, on October 9, 1940, during World War II. When he was 16, he formed a band called the Quarrymen. This band later evolved into the Beatles. Having seen how war can destroy a country, Lennon embraced pacifism as an adult. He tried to spread a message of peace through many of his songs. Lennon was the most political of the Beatles. Many people also think he was the most creative force behind the band. In 1969, he left the Beatles to pursue a solo career.

pacifism: *opposition to war or violence of any kind*

? When Lennon was young, his Aunt Mimi said, "The guitar's all very well as a hobby, John, but you'll never make a living out of it." Lennon ignored her opinion and proved her wrong! What does this say about the importance of following a dream?

John Lennon and Yoko Ono are seen holding one of the posters that they distributed to the world's major cities as part of a campaign protesting the Vietnam War.

WAR IS OVER!

IF YOU WANT IT

STORY BEHIND THE SONG

In 1969, Lennon recorded "Give Peace a Chance" at the Queen Elizabeth Hotel in Montreal, Quebec. The song was recorded during a "Bed-In for Peace." Like the sit-ins of the '60s, a bed-in was a type of nonviolent protest. In 1971, Lennon first recorded "Imagine." Like "Give Peace a Chance," this song also helped Lennon spread his message of peace. This song asked listeners to "Imagine all the people/Sharing all the world."

MEANINGFUL MUSIC

"Imagine" was on the U.S. charts for nine weeks. It achieved the number three spot. Surprisingly, the song's popularity amazed Lennon. He claimed that the lyrics were actually quite radical. "Imagine there's no countries/It isn't hard to do/Nothing to kill or die for/And no religion too." According to Lennon, these words were anti-religious, anti-nationalistic, and anti-capitalist. He said it was the song's "syrupy" melody that helped it become so popular. "Now I understand what you have to do. Put your political message across with a little honey," he once said. Lennon recognized that it was the song's tune, not necessarily its message, that first got people hooked. Once people were listening, they then realized the importance of the lyrics.

sit-ins: *organized, nonviolent protests in which demonstrators peacefully occupy and refuse to leave a place they have been banned from entering*
anti-nationalistic: *not patriotic*
anti-capitalist: *against the private ownership of property, money-seeking, greed, and so on*

The Expert Says...

" ['Imagine' is] an unorthodox anthem that has never been equaled in popular music. "

— Mikal Gilmore, *Rolling Stone* magazine

unorthodox: *breaking with convention or tradition*

10   9   8   7   6

IMAGINE

John Lennon wrote many innovative and interesting songs. He also truly led by example. He used his celebrity status to get his message out to a wide audience. Lennon was passionate about peace. He protested against violence and war. He participated in peace festivals. He hoped these would help to educate the public. Lennon's quest for a better world made him one of our most important musical icons.

After he left the Beatles, Lennon hoped to simplify his art. He also wanted to understand his life more clearly. In his music, he said he hoped to express himself "as simply [and] straightforwardly as possible."

Lennon gave "Imagine" a stirring melody. This tune helped increase interest in the song. However, Lennon's compelling lyrics really got his message across. Today, the song is an international symbol of peace. It is "an enduring hymn of solace and promise that has carried us through extreme grief," according to *Rolling Stone* magazine. "[F]rom the shock of Lennon's own death in 1980 to the unspeakable horror of September 11th," the song has helped the public through many tragic events.

---

solace: *comfort during times of sorrow or misfortune*

Quick Fact

On October 9, 2007, Yoko Ono unveiled the "Imagine Peace Tower" in Reykjavik, Iceland. Lyrics from "Imagine" are engraved at the base of the tower in 24 languages.

Quick Fact

On December 8, 1980, Lennon's brilliant and inspiring life came to a violent end. Lennon, a man who promoted peace, was shot by a crazed fan. His assassin, Mark David Chapman, had asked for his autograph just hours earlier.

? If John Lennon were still alive today, what social or political issues do you think he would write about? Explain your choices.

Take Note

A soulful song, "Imagine" slips into the #5 spot. The simple, poetic brilliance of "Imagine" has made it a favorite for more than 35 years. This song has brought people across the world together. It has inspired people to strive for peace. Its powerful message ranks it higher than "Satisfaction."

• Compare the benefits of being in a band to being a solo musician. Which would you prefer and why?

5   4   3   2   1

RESPECT

Aretha

Aretha Franklin (far right) won eight Grammy Awards in a row for Best Female R&B Vocal Performance starting in 1967 for "Respect."

ARTIST: Otis Redding wrote this song but Aretha Franklin made it famous.

ALBUM AND YEAR: *I Never Loved a Man the Way I Love You*, 1967

A REAL REVOLUTION! Known as the "Queen of Soul," Franklin sang with such skill and passion that she became a voice for African-American pride and women's empowerment.

In 1967, Aretha Franklin established that she was the true Queen of Soul! On Valentine's Day of that year, at Atlantic Records' New York studio, Franklin first spelled out the word R-E-S-P-E-C-T on record. Her backup singers chanted "Sock it to me" at high speed. This powerful version of Otis Redding's "Respect" made it to the #1 spot on the charts. Franklin and the song have been famous ever since.

"Respect" appeared on Aretha Franklin's breakthrough album *I Never Loved a Man the Way I Love You*. This was her first album for Atlantic Records. It was also the first album that highlighted Franklin's background in soul, gospel, and R&B. Thanks to the album's popularity, Aretha Franklin became a superstar!

"Respect" was embraced by the African-American community. "Many also saw Franklin as a symbol of black America itself," says writer Richie Unterberger. According to Unterberger, Franklin was seen as "reflecting the increased confidence and pride of African Americans in the decade of the Civil Rights Movement." This song put what many people were thinking into words. It became Franklin's "most famous track as well as a civil rights and feminist anthem," according to the BBC. For making everyone listen up, this song ranks #4.

RESPECT

Quick Fact

In 1985, Michigan declared Aretha Franklin's voice a natural resource. Just two years later, Franklin became the first female inductee into the Rock and Roll Hall of Fame.

ARTIST BIO

Aretha Franklin was born in Memphis, Tennessee, in 1942. Her mother was a gospel singer. Her father was a minister who was also known for his powerful pipes. Franklin grew up singing gospel music in her father's church. In 1960, she moved to New York City to follow her dream of being a professional singer. Franklin made 10 records between 1960 and 1966. During this time, she only had one hit. It wasn't until "Respect" was released that Franklin's career took off. Since then she has had 20 #1 R&B hits. She has also won 17 Grammy Awards!

STORY BEHIND THE SONG

Otis Redding wrote "Respect." He recorded the song in 1965, two years before Franklin made it a hit. Franklin's version demanded an end to disrespect of every kind. Her powerful vocals made it clear that this wasn't optional. The strength in Franklin's voice caught everyone's attention. Even Otis Redding jokingly said that Franklin had stolen the song "Respect" away from him. Redding wrote it, but Franklin made it famous.

pipes: *vocal chords; voice*

MEANINGFUL MUSIC

"Respect" was released just a few years after the Civil Rights Act of 1964 was passed. This act banned segregation in U.S. schools and public places. Many laws passed during the '60s helped to give African Americans equal rights under U.S. law. "Respect" embodied the feeling of the Civil Rights Movement. Of all of Franklin's work, "'Respect' had the biggest impact," according to music writer Jerry Wexler. The song was "truly global in its influence, with overtones for the Civil Rights Movement and gender equality."

overtones: *associated meanings*

? Franklin's marriage was in crisis when she recorded "Respect." Her producer felt this was why the recording was so passionate: "If she didn't live it, she couldn't give it." In your opinion, is a song more believable if the artist has experienced what he or she is singing about? Explain.

Quick Fact

Aretha Franklin has had the honor of singing at the funerals of some of America's most important civil rights activists. In 1968, she sang at the funeral for Martin Luther King Jr. In 2005, she sang at Rosa Parks's funeral.

Aretha Franklin performs in 2004.

ARETHA FRANKLIN PERFORMS IN 2004—PHOTO BY LISA O'CONNOR/KPA-ZUMA/KEYSTONE PRESS/KEYSTONE

Finding Her VOICE

"Respect" helped Aretha Franklin find her true voice. The song also brought people across America together. It helped people demand the respect they deserved. Read more about Aretha Franklin and her first hit in this article.

It took Aretha Franklin almost a decade to truly find her voice. At Columbia Records, her advisers tried to turn her into a "jazzy pop" singer. Her time at Columbia gave her some experience. But it didn't produce any chart toppers.

After signing with Atlantic Records, Franklin shot to the top of the charts. Songs like "I Never Loved a Man" and, of course, "Respect" had everyone excited. Franklin's new style emphasized her raw, gritty vocals. "With her switch to Atlantic … Aretha proceeded to revolutionize soul music," according to the Rock and Roll Hall of Fame. At this time, she made "some of the genre's greatest recordings." Today, Aretha Franklin is known as the "definitive female soul singer of the '60s," according to *Rolling Stone* magazine. Franklin is also "one of the most influential and important voices in the history of popular music."

With "Respect," Franklin truly became a soul singer. In doing so, she became a voice for the Civil Rights Movement and for women's liberation. By finding her own voice, Aretha Franklin gave a voice to others.

definitive: *best; perfect example*

Quick Fact

Producer John Hammond first heard Aretha Franklin sing in 1960. At the time, he said she had the greatest voice since jazz legend Billie Holiday.

The Expert Says…

"Franklin helped complete the task begun by Billie Holiday and others. … Women were no longer just going to stand around and sing about broken hearts; they were going to demand respect."

— Christopher John Farley, *TIME* magazine

Take Note

"Respect" earns the #4 spot. There's no doubt that John Lennon was a talented singer. However, Franklin sings "Respect" with such passion that she's earned ours. In this song, people heard a demand for equal rights for men and women of all races. For provoking people to demand change, "Respect" ranks higher than "Imagine."

• How would you define respect? In what ways is it important at school, at home, and in everyday life?

5   4   3   2   1

In 1977, Marley released a single called "Punky Reggae Party" to encourage a bond between reggae and punk music. Both genres are about standing up to authority and oppression.

SONG

ARTIST: Bob Marley

ALBUM AND YEAR: *Uprising*, 1980

A REAL REVOLUTION! "Redemption Song" has a powerful political and spiritual message. It speaks to all people and it represents the new sound Marley popularized.

By the time he wrote and recorded "Redemption Song," Bob Marley was already a legend. He was also the first Jamaican artist to become an international superstar. He reached people across the world with his music. And he was only 35 years old.

Throughout his career, Marley used music to educate, empower, and enlighten those around him. "Redemption Song" was no exception. It deals with the oppression of slavery. It also stresses the need for physical and mental freedom. Marley's insights made him a hero to the oppressed. In Jamaica, "he was viewed as a figure of almost mystical proportions," according to writer Jason Ankeny. Many people saw Marley as a type of prophet, or leader.

"Redemption Song" was released in 1980. Bob Marley died just one year later. In 1994, Marley was inducted into the Rock and Roll Hall of Fame. At the time, singer Robert Palmer wrote of Marley that "no one in rock and roll has left a musical legacy that matters more or one that matters in such fundamental ways." Marley used his music to make people aware of the plight of the poor. "Redemption Song" encourages people to fight for freedom, for equality, and for what they believe in.

mystical: *magical; mysterious*
fundamental: *basic; essential*

REDEMPTION SONG

ARTIST BIO

Marley was born on February 6, 1945, in Nine Mile, Jamaica. From a young age, he knew that music was his calling. For most of his early career, Marley sang with a group of local musicians. This group was originally called the Teenagers. Later on, the group's name evolved into the Wailers. The group chose this name because they were "wailing" from the ghetto. The Wailers signed with Island Records in 1972. A year later, they released *Catch a Fire*. This was the first of their albums to be released internationally. People loved Marley's catchy tunes. They also liked the fact that his songs weren't shallow. They promoted justice and truth.

STORY BEHIND THE SONG

During the 1960s, Marley became a follower of the Rastafarian movement. Rastafarians believe that Emperor Haile Selassie of Ethiopia was a messiah. They also reject violence and materialism. "In 1967, [Marley's] music reflected his new beliefs," states the singer's official Web site. "Gone were the [anarchist] anthems; in their place was a growing commitment to spiritual and social issues, the cornerstone of his real legacy." Bob Marley wrote "Redemption Song" in 1979. By this time, he had already been diagnosed with cancer. Despite his illness, he wrote a song full of hope.

messiah: *religious leader; savior*
anarchist: *promotion of disorder or revolt against established rules, laws, and customs*

? Bob Marley died of cancer when he was only 36 years old. What causes do you think Marley might be fighting for if he were alive today? What is it about his message that people find so powerful?

MEANINGFUL MUSIC

"Redemption Song" was a wake-up call to people around the world. The song warns people against the evils of slavery. It inspires people to have faith and not to lose hope. Marley's fame itself was also groundbreaking. "For Jamaicans, the fact that Bob Marley made it big in the outside world is a validation," broadcaster Jeremy Verity once said. Hundreds of years from now, Marley's songs will be as important as they are today, according to reggae historian Roger Steffens. "'Redemption Song' will still be a rallying cry for emancipation from all tyrannies, physical and spiritual."

validation: *sign of approval*
emancipation: *freedom from oppression*
tyrannies: *abuses of authority*

? Jamaican musician Judy Mowatt once said, "When you need to refer to a certain situation or crisis, there will always be a Bob Marley song that will relate to it. Bob was a musical prophet." Why do you think we often turn to music during a crisis?

The Expert Says...

" Even when he was singing about revelation and revolution … there was something redemptive, something sunny, about Marley's outlook. … He was always seeking to bring people together. "

— Christopher John Farley, author of *Before the Legend*

Quick Fact

In 1999, *TIME* magazine voted Marley's 1977 album *Exodus* the best album of the 20th century. The album was honored because "every song is a classic, from the messages of love to the anthems of revolution."

10   **9**   **8**   **7**   **6**

Get Up, Stand Up!

Learn about the deeper meaning of Bob Marley's "Redemption Song" in this article.

Bob Marley was a Rastafarian. He believed that Africans were spread across the world as a result of the slave trade. Rastas believe that a leader will one day guide them back to Africa, their homeland.

In "Redemption Song," Marley wrote that "Old pirates, yes, they rob I / Sold I to the merchant ships." In these lines, Marley remembers how Africans were abducted from their homes. He tells the story of how these people were crammed into the lower decks of ships and taken to other countries to work as slaves. Millions of Africans died on these journeys from disease and starvation. Historians believe that there were over 30,000 slave ship voyages from Africa to America.

In this song, Marley reminds people that they can rise above abuse. "Won't you help to sing / These songs of freedom?" Marley's words remind people that by having faith and by believing in themselves, they can be liberated from things in life that keep them down.

Take Note

Bob Marley lands the #3 spot with "Redemption Song." This quiet, spiritual folk song is by the greatest reggae artist of all time. It is representative of Marley's entire body of work. This song is a very direct plea for justice.

- Bob Marley grew up in a slum outside of Kingston, Jamaica. Is it possible for a privileged person to sing about injustice as genuinely as Bob Marley? Why or why not?

Columbia, Holiday's record label, refused to record "Strange Fruit." The company thought it was too controversial. Holiday turned to Commodore Records, a specialty label, to record the powerful tune.

UIT

ARTIST: Under the pen name Lewis Allen, Abel Meeropol wrote the poem that "Strange Fruit" is based on. Billie Holiday made the song famous.

ALBUM AND YEAR: 1939

A REAL REVOLUTION! "Strange Fruit" was one of the first anti-racism protest songs ever recorded. It became jazz legend Billie Holiday's most well-known song.

When Billie Holiday first performed the song "Strange Fruit," she was met with silence, not applause. It's not that the audience didn't like the song, they were just too stunned to respond. "Strange Fruit" is about murders committed by lynch mobs in the American South during the 1930s.

Holiday first sang this song at New York City's Café Society nightclub in 1939. This was the first club in the city that was open to both African-American and white patrons. Holiday's first performance of the song was a powerful moment. It was so powerful that the club owner asked whether she would sing the song to close all her shows. Holiday found the song emotionally draining. But she knew how important it was and agreed to perform it at every show.

"Strange Fruit" is a song about unspeakable acts committed by racists. This song confronts controversial issues. Since it was first performed, its powerful lyrics have inspired people to fight for change. This song became one of the most influential protest songs ever written, and it directly influenced the Civil Rights Movement of the 1950s and 1960s.

"Strange Fruit" is not your typical song. But it is one of the most revolutionary songs in American history.

---

lynch mobs: *groups with no legal authority that kill people, usually by hanging*

STRANGE FRUIT

ARTIST BIO

Billie Holiday was born Eleanora Fagan in 1915. She created her stage name based on a popular actress's name. Holiday was raised primarily by her mother and rarely saw her father. Because of the family's extreme poverty, she was forced to drop out of school in the fifth grade. When she was 12, she and her mother moved to Harlem in New York City. After numerous struggles, she was discovered by talent scout John Hammond. He thought she had the best singing voice he'd ever heard. Despite her talent, Holiday had to fight against racism and sexism throughout her career.

STORY BEHIND THE SONG

Originally a poem, "Strange Fruit" was written by a Jewish teacher from the Bronx named Abel Meeropol. In 1937, Meeropol was shown a photo of the lynching of two African-American men in Indiana in 1930. He once said that the photo had "haunted him for days." He wrote "Strange Fruit" to express his horror at the lynchings. The poem was first published in *New York Teacher* magazine. Meeropol later put it to music. It was performed several times before it was introduced to Billie Holiday. After she performed it, she admitted that she feared she might be threatened or attacked for performing such a strong protest song.

MEANINGFUL MUSIC

Billie Holiday's mastery of the jazz genre influenced countless musicians. She was a talented singer. But it was the subtle emotional and personal touch she put into each song that made her a legend. Holiday's fame helped "Strange Fruit" reach a wide audience. Thanks to Holiday's recording, the song was embraced by the public. "Strange Fruit" was the "first significant protest in words and music, the first unmuted cry against racism," according to music writer Leonard Feather. For *TIME* magazine, it is simply the best song of the 20th century.

---

unmuted: *not silenced*

In 1943, Esquire magazine voted Billie Holiday the best jazz vocalist of her time.

? Why do you think Holiday feared for her safety after performing this song? Even though she was scared of how people might react to the song, she went ahead and sang it anyway. What does this tell you about Holiday's personality?

Quick Fact

According to the Center for Constitutional Rights, between 1882 and 1968, angry lynch mobs killed 4,743 people in the United States. Over 70% of these people were African Americans.

The Expert Says...

" 'Strange Fruit' tackled racial hatred head-on at a time when protest music was all but unknown. "

— David Margolick, author of *Strange Fruit: The Biography of a Song*

"Strange Fruit" is considered the first real protest song. Read all about the changes that this song inspired in this list of highlights from the Civil Rights Movement.

Rosa Parks: 1955

At this time, local laws often required African Americans to sit at the back of buses. On December 1, 1955, Parks refused to give her seat near the front of a bus to a white passenger. Her arrest sparked the Montgomery Bus Boycott, led by Martin Luther King. On November 13, 1956, the U.S. Supreme Court ruled that segregation on buses was unconstitutional.

Little Rock Integration Crisis: 1957

During the 1950s, many people were fighting to de-segregate schools in the United States. But there were many obstacles on the road to de-segregation. In 1957, the National Guard was ordered to block nine African-American students from entering Little Rock Central High School. It took a court order from President Eisenhower to bring the crisis to an end. After 21 days, he sent in federal troops to escort the students to class. The president's actions dealt "a crushing blow to opponents of the black Civil Rights Movement," according to the BBC.

Greensboro Sit-In: 1960

At this time, many restaurants had "whites-only" policies. This inspired four African-American college students to hold a protest. They sat at the "whites-only" lunch counter of a restaurant in Greensboro, North Carolina. People in other communities copied their peaceful protest. Little by little, restaurants around the country abandoned their segregation policies.

---

unconstitutional: *conflicting with the guidelines of the U.S. Constitution; laws that are declared unconstitutional are struck down*

Take Note

"Strange Fruit" deserves the #2 spot. A powerful protest song, it brought the horrors of prejudice and injustice to light. Like "Redemption Song," this song faces the issue of racism head on. For its direct connection to the Civil Rights Movement, "Strange Fruit" ranks higher.

• The Civil Rights Movement was a time of reform in the United States. Find out more about it. Research a few other historic moments from this time in history.

5   4   3   **2**   1

Bob Dylan has 12 songs on Rolling Stone magazine's list of the top 500 songs of all time. "Like a Rolling Stone" is #1.

ARTIST: Bob Dylan

ALBUM AND YEAR: *Highway 61 Revisited*, 1965

A REAL REVOLUTION! With "Like a Rolling Stone," Bob Dylan brought an electric guitar sound to folk music and poetry to rock and roll.

"I wrote it. I didn't fail. It was straight." This is what Bob Dylan said in 1965 after recording "Like a Rolling Stone." After two frustrating days in a recording studio, the song that would become Dylan's most famous was finally on tape. Al Kooper, who played organ on the recording, once said of the session, "There was no sheet music, it was totally by ear. And it was totally disorganized, totally punk. It just happened." Despite its chaotic beginnings, "Like a Rolling Stone" is the greatest song of all time, according to *Rolling Stone* magazine. Dylan himself once said it is his best song. Out of the hundreds of songs he's written during his career, "Like a Rolling Stone" stands out for its revolutionary sound and content.

"Like a Rolling Stone" was Dylan's first major hit. The song stayed on the charts for longer than two months. At over six minutes long, the song was almost twice the length of most pop songs of the day. It challenged what people thought they wanted to hear on the radio.

This song changed popular music. With this song, Dylan moved from performing folk music to focusing on "in your face" rock and roll. This song's defiant attitude and musical innovation make it the #1 most revolutionary song of all time.

defiant: *bold; gutsy; unwilling to back down*

Like a rolling stone

LIKE A ROLLING STONE

ARTIST BIO

Dylan was born on May 24, 1941 in Duluth, Minnesota. Born Robert Allen Zimmerman, Dylan changed his name when he started performing. He shortened his first name to Bob, and since he liked the poet Dylan Thomas, he chose Dylan as his last name. In 1961, Dylan moved to New York City. He played guitar, keyboard, and harmonica. He also wrote and, despite his unusual voice, performed his own songs. Dylan became known for his folk sound and political protest songs. "These were songs that reflected the tension and unrest of the civil rights and anti-war movements of the '60s," according to CBS News. Through his music, Dylan became a voice for peace and social justice.

? Dylan liked poet Dylan Thomas's work so much that he named himself after the poet! Read some of Thomas's works. How and why do you think these poems inspired Bob Dylan?

Quick Fact

"Like a Rolling Stone" is one of five Bob Dylan songs on the Rock and Roll Hall of Fame's list of 500 Songs that Shaped Rock and Roll. His "Subterranean Homesick Blues," "Blowin' in the Wind," "Tangled Up in Blue," and "The Times They Are A-Changin' " also made the list.

The Expert Says...

" No other pop song has so thoroughly challenged and transformed the commercial laws and artistic conventions of its time, for all time. "

— David Fricke, *Rolling Stone* magazine

conventions: *common practices; customs*

STORY BEHIND THE SONG

The Beatles inspired Dylan to move away from traditional folk sounds. He felt that going electric was the best way to connect with modern audiences. With "Like a Rolling Stone," Dylan also started focusing on more personal topics. The song actually started out as a 24-page short story. The story was about an upper-class girl who falls on hard times. In "Like a Rolling Stone," Dylan uses images to mock posers. Dylan's emphasis on personal songwriting "marks a turning point in [folk music's] 20th-century evolution," according to writer Stephen Erlewine.

? Bob Dylan has been nominated for the Nobel Prize in Literature numerous times. His nomination has sparked debate about whether song lyrics can be considered literature. What do you think? Are lyrics a form of literature? Explain.

MEANINGFUL MUSIC

This song "pierced the consciousness of a whole new generation," according to *TIME* magazine writer Jay Cocks. It made "everyone realize that rock music could be as direct, as personal, and as vital as a novel or a poem." Before this song, many producers and artists believed that people were only interested in three-minute tunes about trivial subjects. With "Like a Rolling Stone," Dylan "proved that complex, intricate lyrics were no barrier to success," according to the BBC.

---

posers: *people who pretend to be something they're not*
trivial: *of very little importance; insignificant*

? Bruce Springsteen once said that the first time he heard a Dylan song, it "sounded like somebody had kicked open the door to your mind." What do you think he meant by this? Describe a song that had this kind of impact on you.

HOW DOES IT FEEL

Read this opinion piece and see whether you agree or disagree with the author's interpretation of Dylan's lyrics.

In the early 1960s, Dylan moved from acoustic to electric guitar, much to the dismay of his folk fans. When he plugged in his guitar at the Newport Folk Festival in 1965, fans were outraged. He was booed off the stage after only three songs! Soon after, he had his first major hit with "Like a Rolling Stone." Dylan revolutionized both the folk and rock genres by blending them into a new musical hybrid. Many Dylan fans feel that "Like a Rolling Stone" was a response to critics who thought he should stick to pure folk. Analyze Dylan's intent in these lyrics.

"HOW DOES IT FEEL
TO BE WITHOUT A HOME"

In these lines, Dylan expresses his confusion at the treatment he received from his former folk fans. He was without a "home" after they booed him off-stage. He was no longer a part of the folk scene but was not clearly defined as a rock star.

"WHEN YOU GOT NOTHING, YOU GOT NOTHING TO LOSE
YOU'RE INVISIBLE NOW, YOU GOT NO SECRETS TO CONCEAL."

After being separated from his original fan base, Dylan had nothing left to lose. As a private person, Dylan may have felt he'd given so much of himself that there was nothing left to "conceal." These lyrics from "Like a Rolling Stone" may have been his turning point from folksinger to revolutionary rock musician.

---

hybrid: *combination of two or more things*

Quick Fact

In 1999, Dylan was named one of the 100 most influential people of the century by *TIME* magazine. Dylan also appeared on *Rolling Stone* magazine's list of the 100 Greatest Artists in history — he was #2.

Take Note

"Like a Rolling Stone" rolls into the #1 spot. With this song, Dylan changed the contemporary American music scene. He proved that he didn't need to have a powerful voice to be popular. Dylan also showed that audiences wanted powerful lyrics with deep meaning. As *TIME* magazine writer Jay Cocks recently wrote, "Bob Dylan couldn't wait for the music to change. He couldn't be only part of the change. He was the change itself."

• What's more important: the music or the message? Describe a musician who has both beautiful vocals and a strong message. What is his or her message?

5   4   3   2   1

We Thought ...

Here are the criteria we used in ranking the 10 most revolutionary songs.

The song:
- Has inspiring lyrics
- Inspired changes in the music industry
- Inspired political change
- Changed how people dressed
- Changed what people listened to
- Launched the career of a revolutionary artist
- Was groundbreaking
- Challenged the rules of its genre